A-Z
PRACTICES

THAT CAN PRESERVE YOUR MARRIAGE

Fatai Kasali

A-Z Practices That Can Preserve Your Marriage

© 2025 Fatai Kasali

The author has asserted his right to be identified as the author of this work in accordance with the Copyright, Designs and Patents Act 1988.

All rights reserved. No part of this publication may be reproduced, stored in a retrieval system, or transmitted, in any form or by any means, electronic, mechanical, photocopying, recording or otherwise without the prior permission of the author.

All Scripture quotations, unless otherwise indicated, are taken from the Holy Bible, King James Version, Cambridge University Press, Oxford University Press, HarperCollins and the Queen's Printers.

Scripture quotations marked 'Phillips' are taken from The New Testament in Modern English, copyright © 1958, 1959, 1960 J.B. Phillips and 1947, 1952, 1955, 1957 The Macmillian Company, New York. Used by permission. All rights reserved.

Published in the United Kingdom by Glory Publishing

ISBN: 978-1-7385361-1-5

INTRODUCTION

God established the institution of marriage to make man fulfil his divine destiny. God made man the head of marriage, while He made woman to be a helpmate for the man. The first couple in Genesis 3 were adults when God married them to each other. Since then, up till now, marriage has always been intended to be established between two adults. This is because marriage involves a lot of responsibilities that can only be handled by adults. To have a successful marriage will require the application of biblical principles.

This book has been written to educate couples about some practical basic principles that can preserve their union. The contents of this book are brief so that couples can read it over within a few hours. Nevertheless, it is recommended that readers go over the contents of this book repeatedly and meditate on it for more understanding and applications.

CONTENTS

A	–	Admission	7
B	–	Boldness	9
C	–	Communication	11
D	–	Dedication	13
E	–	Elevate	15
F	–	Forgiveness	18
G	–	Godliness	20
H	–	Helpfulness	22
I	–	Intentionality	23
J	–	Joy	25
K	–	Keep It Up	27
L	–	Liberty	29
M	–	Management	31
N	–	Narrow It Down	33
O	–	Open-Mindedness	35
P	–	Prayer	37
Q	–	Quit	39
R	–	Reflection	41
S	–	Sensitivity	43
T	–	Thankfulness	45
U	–	Unleash	47
V	–	Visualisation	48
W	–	Word	50
X	–	X-Ray	51
Y	–	Yield	53
Z	–	Zealous	55

A

ADMISSION

Proverbs 28:13 (KJV): *He that covereth his sins shall not prosper: but whoso confesseth and forsaketh them shall have mercy.*

When a partner in a marriage accepts their error, it is evident that they have chosen to personally take responsibility for their mistakes. This is called an admission of mistake or error. Such a partner will not be defensive or deny their mistakes.

In any relationship, a man who refuses to admit his mistakes can never be successful, but if he confesses and forsakes them, he gets another chance.

Admitting when you're wrong quenches anger and prevents the devil from fuelling misunderstanding in relationships.

Even in court, admitting an error or offence reduces punishment. Similarly, God pardons and gives another chance to a person who is quick to admit their wrongdoing and makes an effort to repent.

Admission of offence or mistake softens the heart of the offended partner.

Who can admit his error and apologise to his partner?

1. The humble will admit their errors. This is because it takes humility and brokenness to admit an error. The humblest partner in a relationship is one who is quick to admit a mistake.
2. The wise will admit their errors. This is because it takes the wisdom of God to see where you missed it. Fools don't see their errors, so they keep committing the same mistake over and over again.

3. A right-thinking person will admit their error. This is because only those who can think right will see their errors and admit them.

4. The strong will admit their errors. This is because it takes inner strength to admit your error. Admission of mistake is evidence of strength, not weakness. The strongest among partners is quick to admit their error and is not ashamed to say, 'I was wrong'. The weakest among partners is always defensive because their low self-esteem hinders them from admitting their errors.

5. The courageous will admit their errors because it takes bravery for a person to acknowledge their faults. A courageous partner will admit their mistakes even if they know their partner might treat them with disrespect or look at them differently. They have enough courage to face any embarrassment from such admission.

6. The secured partner will admit their errors. This is because those who feel secured in their relationships quickly admit their errors. After all, they know that their partners will not reject them because of this. They don't feel threatened by any factor.

7. The peace lover. This is because only partners who love peace will be able to admit their errors because, through admission, they want to calm the situation and forge peace in their relationships.

8. The spiritually enlightened will admit their errors. This is because admitting errors requires the light of God to reveal and show you where you went wrong. The partner that carries the light of God will be quick to see and confess their errors. You need divine illumination in your heart and spirit to be able to see your error. A partner of a darkened heart, void of understanding, will not see their error and may even argue blindly to defend themselves.

9. The partner who has the fear of God will admit their errors. This is because such a partner is afraid of God's rebuke. Whenever you refuse to admit you're wrong, you invite God to show you that you were wrong, which comes with punishment. Therefore, the partner who does not want God's rebuke and judgement is quick to admit their error.

B

BOLDNESS

Acts 4:29 (KJV): *And now, Lord, behold their threatenings: and grant unto thy servants, that with all boldness they may speak thy word.*

When fear came against the disciples, they prayed for boldness. This is Spirit-empowered boldness, and it means being brave and courageous.

When negative situations happen in marriage, boldness is required to confront them. When certain situations want to silence you and take away your voice, you need boldness to be able to stand. When life wants to intimidate you in your marriage to take away your self-esteem, you need boldness to stand against it.

When those who have authority over you (such as in-laws, elderly relatives, parents, etc.) are being used by the devil to trouble your marriage, you need boldness to confront and resist them.

When external forces want to take over the running of your home, you need boldness to stand against them.

Similarly, you need boldness to cry for help when your marriage is sinking.

Practice holy boldness, and don't let the devil intimidate you in your marriage. Boldly face every challenge, trouble, intimidation, and attack that the devil wants to throw at your marriage. Do not be shy or pity yourself because of your negative situation. Instead, be bold in God that He will turn things around in your home.

Avoid weeping, crying, self-pity, regret, guilt, intimidation, and any type of fear when challenges come against your marriage. Again, be bold.

Boldly deal with every external or internal force that wants to take over the control of your marriage and disintegrate it. Do not be silent while watching the enemy destroy your home. Boldly deal with every threat coming against your marriage once you identify it. Be bold to resist every attempt of the devil to enter your home through any human vessel. Be bold, but do not be rude.

C

COMMUNICATION

Ephesians 4:29 (KJV): Let no corrupt communication proceed out of your mouth, but that which is good to the use of edifying, that it may minister grace unto the hearers.

Communication is a process or method of exchanging information or messages, which can be verbal or non-verbal.

Marriage can't survive without regular communication, and when communication starts dying in marriage, such a marriage starts dying.

Communication in marriage is an avenue for couples to express their impressions about situations in their homes. It creates opportunities for partners to voice and express their thoughts as regards the affairs of their home. For communication to achieve positive roles in marriage, it must be done in a manner that will not promote strife or misunderstanding between the couple.

Ephesians 4:29 says there should be no corrupt communication. This means couples should avoid using words or expressions that will damage their relationships.

Therefore, for effective communication in marriage, such expressions (verbal or non-verbal) must be:

a. Polite (there should be no insult or attack).
b. Direct (it must be straight to the point).
c. Simple (it should not be complicated).

d. Clear (easy to understand by the listening partner).
e. Safe (it should be done without intimidation and must not cause any injury to the emotion or the mind of the other partner).
f. Gentle (the voice should be soft without being in haste).
g. Respectful (avoid being rude, sarcastic, or irritating the listening partner).
h. Two-way direction (it should not be one-sided communication but let the other partner also speak out).
i. Good body language (be mindful of your gesticulation as you try to express yourself with the movement of your body parts, such as your head, hands, and legs).
j. Blameless (avoid the blame game as you speak because it will open the door for accusations and counter-accusations, which will mess up the discussion).
k. With consent—a mutual agreement (you can't talk to a partner who does not want to listen. Therefore, wisely seek the audience of your partner before you start speaking).
l. Soft voice (avoid being aggressive because this will intimidate the listening partner and make them feel unsafe as you communicate. Similarly, aggressiveness may make your partner misinterpret your statement because your word sounds differently in their ears).
m. Non-corrosive (your word should not be harmful, nor should it cause bad feelings in your partner. Avoid speaking words that could injure your partner's emotions).
n. Be brief as much as possible (too much talk at once confuses the other partner, and they may be unable to absorb or understand the core of your message).

D

DEDICATION

Joshua 24:15 (KJV): *And if it seem evil unto you to serve the LORD, choose you this day whom ye will serve; whether the gods which your fathers served that were on the other side of the flood, or the gods of the Amorites, in whose land ye dwell: but as for me and my house, we will serve the LORD.*

To dedicate your marriage to God implies an act of giving your home to the services of the Lord. It means you consecrate and release your home to be used by the Lord. Whatever is dedicated to the Lord will enjoy special care from the Lord. To secure the future of your marriage, choose to dedicate it to the Lord in service and to promote His glory. Agree with your partner from the onset that you and the children the Lord will give you will serve the Lord and pursue His glory. Ensure that your home is a solid member of a living church where the true word of God is being preached and where you will all grow in the knowledge and fear of God. Let every member of your home serve God in certain capacities and use their gifts and talents to promote the work of the Lord. Make your home usable to the Lord, for the Lord protects whatever is useful to Him.

In Joshua 24:15, Joshua publicly declared that he had dedicated his home to the services of the Lord. This statement from Joshua also revealed his effort to fulfil the conditions of dedicating his family to the Lord. He said his family would not be contaminated with idolatry so that the Lord would accept them as His possession. Therefore, if you choose to dedicate your marriage and home to the Lord, get rid of every contamination from your home. Examples of such contaminations are:

1. **Moral contamination.** Avoid character and behaviour that pollute marriage, such as lies and deception.
2. **Verbal contamination.** Avoid words that pollute marriages, such as abuse and curses.
3. **Spiritual contamination.** Avoid adultery, and don't bring into your home property of devils, such as stolen and accursed things.
4. **Physical contamination.** Avoid fighting or raising hands to strike your partner because this will contaminate and injure their body.
5. **Environmental contamination.** Avoid making your home a dirty place. Cleanliness is next to godliness.
6. **Soulish contamination.** Avoid thoughts and knowledge that will make your mind dirty and make you behave worldly in your marriage.
7. **Emotional contamination.** Avoid creating situations that will make your partner unhappy and sorrowful because God does not dwell in a sorrowful place. He is the God of joy.

E

ELEVATION

Proverbs 4:18 (KJV): *But the path of the just is as the shining light, that shineth more and more unto the perfect day.*

The above Bible verse says the path of the just shines brighter and brighter, which means elevation—things get better and better.

In your marriage, make efforts to make situations get better and better at home and in your relationship.

"To elevate" means to raise to a higher level. You can always do better, no matter how well you and your partners are doing. In your marriage, promote an increase in certain areas of your relationship with your spouse and jointly make an effort to move your relationship forward in many areas.

For a better living with your spouse, examples of things you need to elevate are:

1. **Your knowledge about marriage.** Read more books and listen to more sermons on marriage. Similarly, study the Bible to understand the mind of God about marriage. When you study the Bible, you will be able to know the expectations of God from you and your partner as regards your marriage. The more you know your marital responsibilities, the better you will be able to evaluate your performance in living with your partner.

2. **Your knowledge about your partner.** Make a conscious effort to study your spouse to know them more and more. You can also prayerfully

pursue this. This is because the more you know your spouse, the better you will be living together. Try to know your spouse's temperament, emotions, mindset, life principles, and ideologies. Know the boundaries your spouse has set, their expectations from you, the reasons your spouse got married to you, their gifts, potentials, abilities, weaknesses, vulnerabilities, ambitions, dreams, and visions. Do not live with your spouse as a stranger. Make every effort to understand and know them more and more for a better relationship.

3. **Your knowledge about yourself.** As your spouse has a complicated nature, so do you. Make a conscious effort, if possible, with the help of the Holy Spirit, to study yourself to gain more understanding of who you are.

4. **Study and notice how you react to situations and spoken words from your partner.** Understand how you have been functioning under different situations in your marriage. When you know yourself better, you can then make intentional efforts to control yourself and do better under many situations. Try to know and understand your temperament, emotions, mindset, life principles, and ideologies. Also, know the boundaries you set for your spouse, your expectations from them, the reasons you married them, and your gifts, potentials, abilities, weaknesses, vulnerabilities, ambitions, dreams, and visions.

5. **Your thinking.** There is a direct link between how you think and behave. Make every good effort to improve your thinking system. Grow up in how you think about your partner, yourself, and home. Mature your thinking. In every situation, choose to think in line with the word of God. Meditate on what the word of God says about situations and not what the world or people around you say. Think positively in every situation. Think good and well. Think peace and think progressively. Think about lovely and admirable things always. Think good expectations and think that things will get better with time. Choose not to dwell on wrong thoughts and evil motivations of the heart. If you want to always act good in all situations, choose to think good in all situations because your thinking determines your actions.

6. **Your acts of generosity.** No matter how generous you are to your spouse, you can do better. Move from little to bigger gifts as God

blesses you more and more. Gifts promote peace in relationships, and the more you give to your spouse, the better you will make them happy, creating a peaceful environment at home.

7. **Finally**, for every good thing you do in your marriage, you can always do better and better. Do not be satisfied with the good treatment of your spouse, but aspire to do better and better.

F

FORGIVENESS

Luke 17:1 (KJV): *Then said he unto the disciples, It is impossible but that offences will come: but woe unto him, through whom they come!*

Matthew 6:14-15 (KJV): *For if ye forgive men their trespasses, your heavenly Father will also forgive you: But if ye forgive not men their trespasses, neither will your Father forgive your trespasses.*

In Luke 17:1, Jesus Christ said it is impossible to avoid offences in relationships, but He offered a solution about how to deal with offences. In Matthew 6:14-15, He said we should forgive each other as we offend one another.

Therefore, in your marriage, get ready for offence. Know that you will offend your spouse and vice-versa. As your spouse will offend you, you will also offend your spouse and God. The condition for you to receive forgiveness from God as you offend Him is to also forgive those who offend you.

As offences are certain to come in relationships, the only mitigating factor for them is forgiveness. Forgiveness will not remove the pain or damage the offence has caused but will help make it less severe or painful. It means forgiveness does not totally remove the damage the offence caused, but it helps us to remove or reduce the level of pain it caused.

Offence may cause damage, but with forgiveness, we can reduce or remove the pain level this brings to us. Since time is a healer, with time, we can totally be healed of the damage the offence has caused if we practise forgiveness.

As a Christian family, the kind of forgiveness we should practise in our marriage is forgiveness, that is:

1. **Instant**—you forgive at the same time the offence occurred.
2. **Speedy**—you forgive as if you have been expecting the offence to happen.
3. **Permanent**—it means through forgiveness, you kill that offence in your heart. You will never refer to that offence again in the future.
4. **Perfect**—it means forgiveness leaves no mark of pain or bitterness behind. Even when you remember the offence in the future, you are no longer moved by it anymore. You have allowed time to heal you from the offence done to you by your partner.
5. **Genuine**—it means you are not pretending that you have forgiven but really mean it. There is no more bitterness in your mind about the offence, so it can't influence how you relate with your spouse in the future.
6. **Total**—it means that for every area in which the offence has caused you pain, you will forgive. Sometimes, one offence can touch many areas of your life, such as your career, children, parents, and close associates. However, total forgiveness means that you will no longer focus on any of those areas regarding the offence committed against you.

The above is God's kind of forgiveness, irrespective of the level of seriousness of the offence.

G

GODLINESS

1 Timothy 4:8 (KJV): For bodily exercise profiteth little: but godliness is profitable unto all things, having promise of the life that now is, and of that which is to come.

Godliness is to conform to the character of God. It means couples who desire God's promises to fulfil their union must study God's character and start practising it in their relationships.

The character of God as revealed in the Bible is as follows:

Exodus 34:6-7 (KJV): And the LORD passed by before him, and proclaimed, The LORD, The LORD God, merciful and gracious, longsuffering, and abundant in goodness and truth, Keeping mercy for thousands, forgiving iniquity and transgression and sin, and that will by no means clear the guilty; visiting the iniquity of the fathers upon the children, and upon the children's children, unto the third and to the fourth generation.

From the above, let spouses who want God's promises to be fulfilled in their marriage be:

1. **Merciful to each other.** You must pity your spouse and be compassionate because God is also merciful and compassionate to us.
2. **Gracious to each other.** It means being kind, generous, warm, and giving each other special treatment. Let your spouse always find favour with you as you do with God.
3. **Practise long-suffering.** It means to bear each other's weaknesses for a long time without complaint. In marriage, long-suffering is a lifetime

because as long as you are alive, God will continue to practise long-suffering with you, bearing your weaknesses and faults and always forgiving you. Do the same with your spouse as long as both of you are alive and married.

4. **Be abundant in goodness.** It means you keep doing good for your spouse without limits or preconditions. Never stop being good to your spouse, regardless of whether they deserve it.

5. **Be abundant in truth.** It means telling your spouse the truth in all situations and never lying or deceiving your spouse. Don't hide any fact from your spouse; tell them all that they need to know. The more you know, the more you should tell your spouse. Let your spouse know everything in your heart. Never lie and never deceive.

6. **Always keep mercy for your spouse.** It means being quick to show mercy to your spouse and forgiving them as if you had anticipated their offence.

7. **Practise justice.** Be fair and impartial to your spouse. Don't treat your spouse less favourably compared with other people in your life. Do not maltreat your spouse in order to please your close relatives or any other associates.

H

HELPFULNESS

Galatians 6:2 (KJV): Bear ye one another's burdens, and so fulfil the law of Christ.

The above Bible verse encourages us to be a burden bearer to our spouses. It implies supporting your spouse in carrying their burdens, troubles, or challenges. This requires intentionally seeking the good of your spouse in all situations. It also involves opening your ears to the cry of your spouse as you are moved into action as regards their pain. Be a helpful partner to your spouse. Be a strength to your spouse when they are in need or in a weak position. Be always supportive.

A helpful spouse is a refuge from storms. They are a hiding place when troubles come. They are shadows to the heat as they provide comfort for their spouse when the days are dark. A helpful spouse defends their spouse against the attack of the enemy.

If you make yourself a helpful partner to your spouse, you will stay in the memory of your spouse forever because people don't forget those who help them to succeed in life. By being a helpful partner to your spouse, you will create a space that another person in your spouse's life can never fill. You will become irreplaceable in the life of your spouse, as it will become difficult for your spouse to do without you while you are still alive. If you can be a helpful partner to your spouse, you will make yourself so relevant to your spouse that you will indeed become a helpmate to him or her.

If you want to preserve your marriage, be a helpful partner to your spouse and always be ready to stretch your helping hand to your spouse when they are in need. You can help your spouse build a career, take care of domestic work, pursue dreams and visions, and perform a difficult task. This strengthens the bond in a relationship.

I

INTENTIONALITY

Ephesians 5:15-16 (KJV): *See then that ye walk circumspectly, not as fools, but as wise, Redeeming the time, because the days are evil.*

To be intentional means to be deliberate, voluntary, and willing.

To preserve your marriage deliberately, make the best use of your time with your spouse.

Intentionality teaches us the following:

1. We should set goals and see them through to the end to achieve a purpose; otherwise, we will never achieve our goals.
2. We must be ready to invest our resources to achieve our purpose. Invest your time, money, energy, and every necessary resource to fulfil your purpose. Otherwise, your purpose will remain elusive.
3. We have to work and make practical efforts to deal with issues troubling our relationship; otherwise, those issues will remain.
4. We should know that good things don't happen by accident or chance but by deliberate acts of men.
5. We can't keep doing the same wrong thing and expect different results.
6. Unless we make practical efforts to cause the desired changes, such changes will never happen.

Until spouses discipline themselves and make practical efforts to improve their relationships, things will never be better. It will always be the same old—the same arguments, errors, fights, accusations, counter-accusations, queries, complaints, and anger.

Couples that are not intentional will always have the same issue repeating itself in their relationship until they arise and start making practical efforts to deal with it. For example, if you and your spouse have been fighting over money for years without resolving it, this implies that you have not intentionally made practical efforts to deal with it.

J

JOY

Proverbs 17:22 (KJV): *A merry heart doeth good like a medicine: but a broken spirit drieth the bones.*

To bring joy into your marriage will require a deliberate effort to do something that will make your spouse happy and rejoice.

Proverbs 17:22 states that joy has healing power. It implies that if you want to keep your spouse in good health, do things that will make them happy or rejoice.

Examples of things you can do to make your spouse happy and rejoice in order to promote their well-being are:

1. Do things you know your spouse likes, such as preparing their favourite meal or giving them gifts you know they like.
2. Celebrate your spouse on important dates like marriage anniversaries, birthdays, special achievements, etc.
3. Always speak nice words to the ears of your spouse.
4. Love your spouse until your spouse feels loved.
5. Find out the love language of your spouse and speak it regularly.
6. Spend quality time with your spouse always.
7. Pursue your spouse's interest in all situations—like what your spouse likes and hate what your spouse hates, as much as it is biblical.
8. Pursue your spouse's development, such as in career, ministry, life ambition, etc.

9. Verbally express appreciation to your spouse.
10. Make your spouse feel valuable in your life.
11. Occasionally give your spouse pleasant surprises. Examples of such surprises include birthday party surprises, gifts, nice treatments, etc.

K

KEEP IT UP

1 Corinthians 15:58 (KJV): *Therefore, my beloved brethren, be ye stedfast, unmoveable, always abounding in the work of the Lord, forasmuch as ye know that your labour is not in vain in the Lord.*

To be steadfast means to keep doing the right things. When you keep doing the right things after a long time, it becomes a habit, and habits become a character, and character determines destiny.

In order to preserve your marriage and keep troubles away from your home, you have to keep doing the right things that promote such security in your home. Never stop doing the right things in your home.

Examples of things you need to keep up in your relationship are:

1. Things that you know are making God happy about your marriage.
2. Things that promote peace in your marriage.
3. Prices you pay that make your home stand.
4. Things that make your spouse proud of you.
5. Things you do that make your spouse respect and honour you more.
6. Things that promote the well-being of your marriage.
7. Things that, when you do, enhance the advancement of your home.
8. Things that, when you do, strengthen the bond between you and your spouse.

9. That strength in you that is benefiting your home.
10. That grace you carry that is benefitting your marriage.
11. Those secrets God has revealed to you that are helping you maintain the well-being of your marriage.
12. Those lessons you have learnt over the years that are helping you to live peacefully with your spouse.
13. Those things that, whenever you do them, captivate your spouse, making them give you favourable attention.
14. Those things you discovered that, whenever you give them to your spouse, make them laugh and rejoice.
15. Those things you have noticed that, whenever you do them, help your spouse recover quickly from bad moods and lift their spirits.

Never stop doing the right things in your relationship because when you stop doing them, bad things will start to happen.

L

LIBERTY

Galatians 5:1 (KJV): *Stand fast therefore in the liberty wherewith Christ hath made us free, and be not entangled again with the yoke of bondage.*

Liberty is the power to do as one pleases without any constraint. Sometimes, in marriage, you know the right things to do to make your spouse happy, but some constraints could prevent you from doing such things. You must fight and remove whatever will not let you do the right things concerning your marriage.

Examples of things that may constrain you from doing the right things are:

1. **Guilty conscience.** This hinders your liberty to act in certain ways. Enemies will keep reminding you of the wrong you did to your spouse, suggesting that your spouse may not have genuinely forgiven you. Do not let a guilty conscience keep you from doing the right things.

2. **Self-condemnation.** Sometimes, you will find it hard to forgive yourself for the error you committed, which may prevent you from making another good effort that will benefit your marriage next time. If you have done wrong before, it does not mean you will always be doing wrong. Be quick to forgive yourself whenever you make a mistake and promptly decide to move on with your life.

3. **Fear of failure from the past.** If you want to try again for good things you once failed to achieve for your family, the devil may remind you that you will not succeed again. The devil would like to exploit your

past mistakes to cage you so that you will not make another effort. Do not let fear cage you and prevent you from doing things that benefit your marriage.

4. **Offence of the past.** If your spouse has done you wrong in the past or disappointed you in the past, and you want to trust him or her again, the devil will remind you of those past disappointments, giving you enough reasons you should not do it again. Do not let the offence of the past take away your liberty to trust your spouse.

5. **Fear of rejection.** If your spouse once rejected you for certain things, and you want to make another attempt, the devil will remind you that you will be rejected again, so don't try it. Temporary rejection does not equate to permanent rejection.

6. **Fear of misinterpretation.** If you once had a problem with your spouse due to misinterpretation of what you said or did and want to make another attempt, the devil will remind you that you will be misinterpreted again. The more you let this stop you, the more you lose effective communication in your marriage.

The more you allow these negative reminders to control your actions, the more likely you will lose your liberty in your marriage. You have to refuse to be the prisoner of your past.

M

MANAGEMENT

1 Peter 4:10 (KJV): *As every man hath received the gift, even so minister the same one to another, as good stewards of the manifold grace of God.*

Stewardship means management of whatever is put in your custody.

For a successful marriage, you have to learn how to manage the following:

1. Yourself in terms of emotion, reasoning, how you view things, react to situations, etc. Learn how to put yourself under control in all situations without permitting the devil to cause trouble in your marriage.
2. Your spouse's emotions, reactions, and how they handle situations at home.
3. Your children's emotions, reactions, gifting, talents, potentials, abilities, and disabilities.
4. External people related to your marriage, such as parents, in-laws, friends, and other associates. Learn how to manage and effectively control their excesses so that the devil will not use them to destroy your marriage.
5. Family resources such as money, properties, and other possessions that belong to your family. Avoid wastage.
6. Affairs of your home, such as parenting, family projects, careers, and other plans of the family. Manage them without becoming an agent of hindrance to your family's progress.

7. Trials and challenges coming against your marriage. This may include health challenges, debt, joblessness, economic problems, and any other discomfort against your home. Manage them well without expanding the problems.
8. Abundance such as an overflow of blessings—learn how to save your leftovers for the rainy days.
9. Family secrets. Some family matters are extremely confidential, and you should not even let your parents become aware of them.
10. Time. You must learn how to manage your time so that you will have time for your spouse and children.

Failure to effectively manage family matters may pave the way for the devil to cause greater troubles.

N

NARROW IT DOWN

Proverbs 4:25 (KJV): Let thine eyes look right on, and let thine eyelids look straight before thee.

When your eyes look straight, it means you will lose some focus—you will not be able to see certain things well.

To narrow down your focus means you don't pay attention to everything happening around you concerning your marriage.

In marriage, to avoid distractions, there are things you will need to intentionally ignore and not give your attention to.

In order to narrow down your focus, you will need to differentiate between major and minor. Some things are essential, while others are less important. Focus on the major things and leave behind minor stuff.

Focus only on major situations you can handle, and entrust those significant matters beyond your control to God. Don't do what only God can do; otherwise, you will be worn out.

Narrowing down your focus is necessary so that you don't wear yourself out, and moreover, because you don't have all the strength.

Learn to ignore certain wrong things your spouse may have done to you. Don't pay attention to every wrong thing your spouse does to you. Be mature enough to overlook some offences. Learn how to ignore some words said to you because your spouse is a human being, and many times, we don't attach importance to many words we say, nor do we know their full implication on the hearers.

Know that some things don't deserve your attention; therefore, just ignore them. For the sake of peace, narrow your focus and don't give your attention to everything you see or hear in your relationship with your spouse.

O

OPEN-MINDEDNESS

2 Corinthians 6:11 (KJV): *O ye Corinthians, our mouth is open unto you, our heart is enlarged.*

An enlarged heart is a heart that can accommodate many wrong treatments without developing a negative mindset or expectations.

Whatever error or wrong is done to a person with an enlarged heart will not stain his heart or make him develop a negative mindset and expectations.

To approach your marriage with an open mind means to avoid making prejudgments about situations in your marriage, especially based on wrongs that might have happened in the past. Don't judge a situation or your spouse before an act is done. Stop being a prophet of doom in your marriage. Stop forecasting evil. Learn how to handle each day as it comes.

Avoid making a wrong assumption or negative expectation based on whatever wrong that might have happened in the past in your marriage.

Stop predicting wrong from your spouse. Give them a new chance to prove themselves in every new situation.

Be open to new ideas, advice, wisdom, or suggestions to run your home. Embrace new knowledge as long as it agrees with the word of God. Open your mind to the infinite possibilities God can do in the affairs of your home. God can change a bad spouse into a good one and turn stubborn children into good children. Stop making wrong conclusions in your heart about any incident that has yet to develop.

Many married partners have become negative because they don't approach new things with an open mind. They always forecast evil outcomes in every situation. Whatever happens in your marriage, avoid saying that your partner can never change for the better. Avoid always predicting negatively about anything that concerns your home.

P

PRAYER

Jeremiah 33:3 (KJV): *Call unto me, and I will answer thee, and shew thee great and mighty things, which thou knowest not.*

According to the above Bible verse, when you call unto the Lord regarding your marriage, He will show you things you don't know about your marriage.

To preserve your marriage, you must know things about your spouse, children, yourself, and relations.

Many marriages perish or scatter because couples lack the relevant knowledge necessary to make them succeed. There is certain information you can gain about your marriage, spouse, children, yourself, and family relations that will make you approach situations in your home differently.

One of the reasons we get many things wrong in our marriage is because we base most of our decisions solely only what we know, and often, what we don't know are the factors that really affect our marriage. If you are able to know what you don't know about your marriage, you will get many things right. If you can know what makes your spouse do or say things he or she does or says, your reaction will probably be different.

Therefore, whenever certain incidents occur between you and your spouse, before applying any method, first ask God in prayer to reveal what you need to know about that situation and what steps you should take. You will be amazed when God reveals many things about that situation you did not know before. It is wise to be cautious when judging your spouse's actions and words because many factors in their life may influence them.

Therefore, before you take any action whenever certain incidents happen between you and your spouse, pray that God will reveal every revelation, secret, knowledge, and understanding of all you need to know to make the right decisions.

Q

QUIT

Hebrews 3:13 (KJV): *But exhort one another daily, while it is called To day; lest any of you be hardened through the deceitfulness of sin.*

The Bible verse above indicates that 'today' matters in your relationship with your spouse. It means that delays can be dangerous in certain situations. Delays in repentance for wrongdoings and making the necessary amendments can create more problems in your relationship. This is because the more you delay taking necessary action, the more difficult it will become in the future to take such action. Delays allow wrong things to take deep root in the heart, making bad habits difficult to repent of. There are things you need to quit now before they bring irreparable damage to your marriage.

Examples of such things are:

1. **Associates that hate your spouse.** Whoever hates your spouse or any of your children is your number one enemy. This is because those who hate your family will gradually turn your heart against your family and influence you to hate them yourself. Those who genuinely like you must like the spouse with whom you share your life. Therefore, before these haters of your family become a vessel the devil will use against your home, quickly quit that association.

2. **Job that will make you always unavailable to your spouse and children.** Such a job will destroy your marriage, and when the job ends, you will not have a home to return to after retirement. Therefore, quit now any

job that is always taking you away from your family before you lose your marriage and home.

3. **Things that always cause disagreements and fights between you and your spouse.** Even if you are always right, for the sake of peace, just quit such actions; otherwise, it may become an access for the devil to scatter your marriage.

4. **Association with people who hold different views about Christian marriage.** If you can't quit, distance yourself from such people; otherwise, they may influence you negatively against your marriage. Do not draw too close to your home those who hold views, opinions, principles, and ideologies about marriage that are different from that of Christianity.

5. **Habit that can threaten your health or the health of members of your home.** Examples of such habits include adultery, smoking, alcohol, etc. Do not endanger your life and that of those in your family with self-destructive lifestyles.

6. **Relationship with people that have become thorns in the flesh of your marriage.** People that always trouble your home must not come close to your marriage anymore; otherwise, the devil will use them to vomit unimaginable trouble in your home.

7. **Dreams and personal ambitions that have become a threat to your marriage.** God will never give you a dream or life ambition that will destroy your marriage. Any dream, vision, or ambition that will threaten the well-being of your marriage must go.

If the well-being of your marriage is your priority, prayerfully consider many other things you need to quit for the sake of your marriage.

R

REFLECTION

2 Corinthians 3:18 (KJV): *But we all, with open face beholding as in a glass the glory of the Lord, are changed into the same image from glory to glory, even as by the Spirit of the Lord.*

Reflection is to give serious thought and consideration to something. It includes setting time aside to meditate on something you have done, said, or are about to say or do. Reflection helps us discover hidden details we missed when we did or said something. It is a deeper form of learning that allows us to discover why something took place, why we did what we did, what the impact of our word and action will be on us or the people affected, and whether such things should happen again or not.

Under reflection, the Holy Ghost will help you to discover what you are doing wrong in your marriage, and He will bring conviction to your heart about your behaviour.

Reflection is like an image you see in a mirror. The word of God is our mirror, and when we stand before it, we will see ourselves clearly.

Therefore, under the illumination of the Holy Spirit, reflect on your way of doing things, reasoning, manner of speaking, and how you communicate with your spouse. Meditate on how you have been conducting your home affairs. Spend time before God to let the Holy Spirit expose and reveal who you are to yourself.

Do not just keep going and repeating the same error over and over. Do a regular self-reflection because it enables the Holy Ghost to call your attention to certain things you are doing out of ignorance. There are blind spots in life, but self-reflection allows us to detect them. Learn to take a break to reflect and look back on your past steps to see if they are in the right direction.

S

SENSITIVITY

Hebrews 5:13-14 (KJV): For every one that useth milk is unskilful in the word of righteousness: for he is a babe. But strong meat belongeth to them that are of full age, even those who by reason of use have their senses exercised to discern both good and evil.

Sensitivity means the ability to discern situations. To increase your sensitivity in your relationship with your spouse, you will need to study them, meditate on how your spouse functions under different situations, and also regularly study the word of God under the illumination of the Holy Ghost. The Holy Ghost will then begin to teach you more and more about your spouse and yourself. This will help you build sensitivity as regards your relationship with your spouse.

Spiritual sensitivity and discernment will help you to:

1. Detect the feelings of your spouse without telling you. A sensitive spouse will detect when they have their spouse's feelings and emotions. It also helps you to know when your spouse is not happy without telling you.
2. Discover your spouse's needs without telling you.
3. Discover the evil that Satan has assigned against your marriage before it comes into fulfilment.
4. Predict where your marriage is heading without anyone telling you. Sensitivity will help you to detect signals being sent to you regarding where your marriage is going in life.

5. Detect your wrongs before they cause trouble and major damage to your marriage.
6. Detect signs and signals of underlying problems concerning your marriage before the situation goes out of control.

Generally, before a partner initiates divorce, some vital signs must have been ignored. Sensitivity will help you to quench a problem before it is fully matured. You must become proactive because you have privileged information about the situation.

T

THANKFULNESS

Proverbs 17:13 (KJV): *Whoso rewardeth evil for good, evil shall not depart from his house.*

To show thankfulness means to show gratitude and appreciation to those who have been a blessing to you. In marriage, saying 'thank you' to your spouse when they did something good for you means you are not taking your spouse for granted, nor are you claiming entitlement that your spouse must do you good.

Showing thankfulness to your spouse will make them feel like they are not being used in the relationship. It will also make them feel valued and develop a sense of importance, which is good for their self-esteem.

The more you say 'thank you' to your spouse, the more you help him or her improve his or her self-esteem and self-image.

Without thankfulness, you make your spouse feel like a fool whenever they do you good. Practise appreciation to God and your spouse. Be grateful for every little thing your spouse did for you. A grateful heart will draw more blessings from people. Appreciation encourages people to do more and to please one's grateful spouse. Always say 'thank you' to your spouse for being part of your journey in life. This will also encourage and make them feel valued in that relationship.

U

UNLEASH

Philippians 4:13 (KJV): I can do all things through Christ which strengtheneth me.

The above Bible verse indicates that as a believer, the Lord has loaded you with plenty of potential and giftings to excel in all you do.

To unleash means to release the hidden treasures God has deposited inside you.

In Genesis 3, when God calls Eve a suitable helper for Adam, it means He has deposited treasures within her that will enable her to fulfil her role in Adam's life.

Similarly, God brought you into this marriage because He has deposited inside of you such special abilities, skills, talents, giftings, and potentials that you will need to succeed in your marriage. God has brought you into this marriage so that you can use divine deposits inside of you to bring improvement and fulfilment of destiny to your spouse. Therefore, whenever challenges come against your marriage, the first thing is to look inward because there is potential inside of you that you brought into your marriage for a day like this.

In many situations, God creates avenues for you to discover and unleash your hidden potential by allowing certain challenges to come against your home. Life challenges enable us to discover our giftings and use them for our benefit. When trouble comes against your home, it is an opportunity for you to unleash your hidden potential. Do self-discovery to discover the hidden potential God has deposited inside you for your marriage's sake.

V

VISUALISATION

Genesis 15:5 (KJV): *And he brought him forth abroad, and said, Look now toward heaven, and tell the stars, if thou be able to number them: and he said unto him, So shall thy seed be.*

God asked Abraham to look at the stars and that his seeds shall be numberless like the stars.

Visualisation is the formation of a mental image of something. It allows you to see the future before it happens.

Visualisation is the vision you develop about what your marriage will become in the future.

You will need to always ask yourself the following questions about your marriage:

1. Which kind of products do I want my marriage to produce in the future?

2. Which kind of children do I want my marriage to produce in the future?

3. Which kind of person do I want my spouse to become in the future?

4. Which kind of person do I want my marriage to turn me into in the future?

5. Which kind of testimonies do I want my marriage to produce in the future?

When you are able to answer the above questions, you will be able to decide how you will channel the resources and energy of your marriage. Vision gives direction, and couples who have vision don't waste their time on irrelevant things because they are busy chasing their visions.

Visualisation will help you avoid wasting resources, energy, time, and other treasures God has given your family.

The truth about life is that whether you decide what your marriage will become in the future or not, your marriage will become something, but if you fail to decide what your marriage will become, life will determine it for you. Some marriages have become what the couples don't like because they fail to develop it intentionally, so life does it for them. We will all become something in the future, but if we fail to decide who we will become in the future, life will do it for us.

Therefore, visualise what you want your marriage to become in the future, and start to channel effectively every resource and opportunity life brings on the way of your family to pursue your vision.

W

WORD

Proverbs 18:21 (KJV): *Death and life are in the power of the tongue: and they that love it shall eat the fruit thereof.*

According to the above Bible verse, with the word of your mouth, you can speak death or life into your marriage. With your word, you can make your spouse become motivated or demotivated, develop low or high self-esteem, live a life of hope or hopelessness, belief or disbelief in themselves, etc.

Words can tear a person apart emotionally, mentally, and psychologically. Word can plant good or bad things inside a person. Word can bring out bad or good treasures stored inside a person.

With your word, a demon or an angel of the Lord can start attending to situations in your home.

Therefore, mind your speech because your words can shape the future of your marriage. Word can build and destroy.

Every marital situation can be traced directly or indirectly to the words you and your spouse speak continually at home. In the spirit world, words are no joke because every word is taken seriously and serves as material for manufacturing certain outcomes for the family. Evil words spoken continuously are raw materials for demons to produce evil products for the family. Many couples suffer from sickness due to the kind of word they speak at home. Similarly, many couples thrive in their relationships because of the kind of words they speak to each other. If you want to preserve your marriage, mind your word.

X

X-RAY

1 Corinthians 11:31 (KJV): *For if we would judge ourselves, we should not be judged.*

The above Bible verse says that if we judge ourselves, we will not be judged anymore.

To judge yourself is in terms of your intention and motive for all you do in your marriage.

X-ray is a type of radiation that can go through many solid substances to reveal the hidden object inside it.

When you x-ray things, you reveal hidden and unseen parts of them.

Similarly, when you x-ray your intention to get married, you will expose hidden and secret reasons regarding why you married. Your spouse can't see these hidden and secret reasons, but you know within yourself. These reasons will determine how you relate to your spouse and how you handle situations in your marriage.

- Why do you do what you do in your marriage?
- Why do you act as you always do in your marriage?
- Why do you treat your spouse the way you do?
- Why do you make so many decisions in your marriage?
- What are your expectations for marrying the person you married?

- What are your motives for behaving the way you do in your marriage?
- When you intentionally x-ray your motives for all that you do in your marriage, then you can provide accurate answers to the above questions.

Check it out within yourself if your intention and motives for all you do in your marriage are right biblically.

Y

YIELD

1 Corinthians 9:22 (KJV): *To the weak became I as weak, that I might gain the weak: I am made all things to all men, that I might by all means save some.*

To yield means being able to adjust and become flexible. It means to be open to new things and conditions.

Unyielding people are rigid, inflexible, and unable to fit into a new thing.

Marriage is very dynamic, and rigid partners don't fit into the new days in their marriage, and such partners become very odd and unsuitable to stay in that marriage.

Some partners are highly unreasonable because no matter the level and magnitude of reasons to change such partners, they don't change. They stay in their own corners.

To such a rigid partner, it is either their spouse leaves them behind, or they drag the other partner backwards.

Many rigid partners have left their marriages because they can no longer fit into their homes. While everyone has moved on, they remain behind, expecting others to come and stay with them in their little corner.

Rigid partners are usually an agent of retardation in marriages.

When you notice that you can no longer fit into your marriage, it may be because you refuse to adapt to changing times. As a result, your partner might decide to leave to avoid being tied down by your unwillingness to adjust.

In order to create a progressive home, get ready to change your life principles, ideologies, beliefs, and the doctrines you are using to run your life.

Get ready to move your goalpost for the sake of peaceful co-existence with your family. If your spouse keeps complaining about certain habits of yours, get ready to change. Don't say this is who I am; you have to accept who I am. Truly, this is who you are, but the wisdom of God says that if being yourself will trouble your marriage, be ready to change and become a better version of yourself.

Yielding makes you simple; therefore, avoid being a complicated and complex human being. In order to preserve your marriage, accept a simple apology and explanation. Make yourself simple and easy to live with and relate to.

Z

ZEALOUS

Romans 12:11 (KJV): *Not slothful in business; fervent in spirit; serving the Lord;*

To be zealous is to be warm, enthusiastic, willing, energised, and motivated towards a course. To be zealous or non-zealous is infectious.

A partner who is always cold towards a good course will soon make their spouse likewise cold.

If you truly desire positive changes in your marriage, you will show it through zeal, and your spouse will likely catch the same fire when you do this. The two of you will begin to work together to cause the desired change in your relationship.

Lukewarm partners are always snobbish and uninteresting to live or work with. Get passionate about your relationship with your spouse, and you will ignite a fire of motivation in your relationship.

Books From the Same Author

Journey to the Next Level

The New Creature

Building a Glorious Home:
A Pathway to a Successful Marriage

Enemy of Marriage

Words That Heal

The Winning Formula

Faith that Always wins

Common Mistakes Parents make about their Children

Recovery is Possible
When you are desperate for a miracle

Decision
Path way to a wise decision making

Stop your fear before it stops you

The Visionary

30 Covenant Right Prayers of Declaration That Can Change Your Life

I Am Highly Favoured

This book, and all these other books from the same author, are available at Christian bookstores and distributors worldwide.

They can also be obtained through online retail partners such as Amazon or by contacting the author at the address below:

Address: 21-23 Stokes Croft, Bristol BS1 3PY United Kingdom

Email: kkasali@yahoo.com

Telephone: +44 (0) 7727 159 581

www.ingramcontent.com/pod-product-compliance
Lightning Source LLC
Chambersburg PA
CBHW061741070526
44585CB00024B/2767